TRAINS

Unit Study Guide

By:

Amanda Bennett

OTHER BOOKS BY AMANDA BENNETT:

OCEANS: Unit Study Guide

FLIGHT: Unit Study Guide

SPACE: Unit Study Guide

Bendt Family Ministries   **333 Rio Vista Court**   **Tampa, FL 33604**

TRAINS

Table of Contents

Pages like this have been included for your use to record notes, resources, ideas, children's art work, diagrams or whatever you wish to record from the unit study. Enjoy!

TRAINS -- INTRODUCTION

The distant wail of a train whistle through the still night air -- where is it heading and who is along for the ride? One of the most romantic and nostalgic periods in the history of America involves the development of rail transportation. The lure of the unknown territory and all of its promise of wealth and adventure -- it was enough to make men take great risks with their futures to get the rail throughout the West. What would America be like today without the coming of age of locomotives and rail systems?

As we venture forth with the early inventors and transportation development, we will gain an understanding of man's need to trade with others, try to improve himself as well as support his family. The idea of using steam and rails to move freight has an interesting history that you and your family will enjoy.

This study has been developed to cover the following topics:

- History of freight transportation

- Harnessing of steam in an engine

- How a train engine works

- Using steam engines on trains

- History of American railroads

- Trains and rail systems

- Effects of trains on our lives today

The study of trains and their history is fascinating. You will learn about inventiveness, commitment and willingness to try new ideas. One of the lessons that can be learned from this study is that man can be very creative when a problem arises -- he is only limited by his curiosity and ideas! God gave us amazing brains and abilities, we just have to use them.

TRAINS -- OUTLINE

I. History of Transportation in Early America

    A.   Early transportation

        1.   Ocean crossing by sailing ships
        2.   Ships provided transport between coastal cities
        3.   Colonists used canoes to travel inland

    B.   Colonial transportation

        1.   As American colonies grew, roads inland began to develop.
        2.   Covered wagons became the main source of transportation inland along these rough roads.
        3.   Settlers began crossing the Eastern mountain ranges, and wagons could not be used for goods.
        4.   Pack horses were used along the mountain trails -- limiting the amount of goods that could be moved at one time.

    C.   Early 1800's transportation

        1.   Improvement of Roads

            a.   The Lancaster Pike was built -- the first good road leading to the West.
            b.   Coastal roads improved for moving freight -- water transportation was still more affordable.

        2.   Water transportation routes were improved

            a.   Rivers were cleared of barriers
            b.   Canals were dug for barges to move goods
            c.   The Erie Canal was put into service in 1825, connecting the coastal areas to the inland developments
                (1)   Four feet deep and forty feet wide

    (2) Barges could move freight in one fourth of the time that wagons took.

    (3) Freight rates dropped from $100 to $5 per ton.

    (4) New York City grew rapidly as a result of this trade access

  D. Introducing the steam engine to America

    1. Other towns along the coast did not have inexpensive inland freight transportation -- they were limited by mountains and sought an alternative.

    2. Americans turned to the inventor James Watt and his invention -- the steam engine, for a way to move goods for less cost.

    3. The first steam engine locomotive was used to transport coal for a canal company.

    4. The first commercial train was put into service in 1830 in Charleston, South Carolina by the South Carolina Canal & Railroad Company.

II. The railways grow with America

  A. The railways played a major role in America's Industrial Revolution, providing faster and more reliable freight transportation, and also fueling rapid industrial expansion to all parts of our country.

  B. When the Civil War was fought, it marked the first use of railroads in American conflicts. The railroads were used to move troops and supplies, but the South had numerous weaknesses in its rail system.

  C. The first Transcontinental Railway was completed in 1869, connecting the Union Pacific and Central Pacific tracks, spanning the continent.

  D. Government introduces a land grant program encouraging westward growth and providing the government with a 50% discount on freight rail charges.

E. Fortunes were made with the railroad and the leading development companies.

F. The Depression brought financial failure all across the country, and the railroads were no exception, leading to the collapse of many of the companies.

G. The World Wars helped revive the railroad industry and aid in the recovery of American economy.

H. With declining mail and passenger service in 1971, Congress formed Amtrak to handle intercity passenger service, supporting commuter service.

III. Developers of the railway

A. Richard Trevithick -- built a steam engine that could do work, moving loads

B. George and Robert Stephenson -- developed the *ROCKET* steam locomotive and won The Rainhill Trials, changing forever the design of steam locomotives.

C. Thomas Brassey -- most successful railway builder, amassing a fortune.

D. George Pullman -- furniture-maker that designed and built a luxury railway car for comfortable travel.

E. Thomas Cook -- ran the first "railway excursion" for train passengers.

F. George Westinghouse -- invented the air brake, railroad frog, and a complete railroad signal system.

G. George Pullman -- developed the sleeping car for railway travel.

IV. Legends and heroes of the railway

A. Kate Shelley -- brave girl who saved hundreds of lives when a storm in Iowa washed out a train trestle.

B. Casey Jones (John Luther Jones) -- railway engineer who saved others by sacrificing his own life to avoid a major collision.

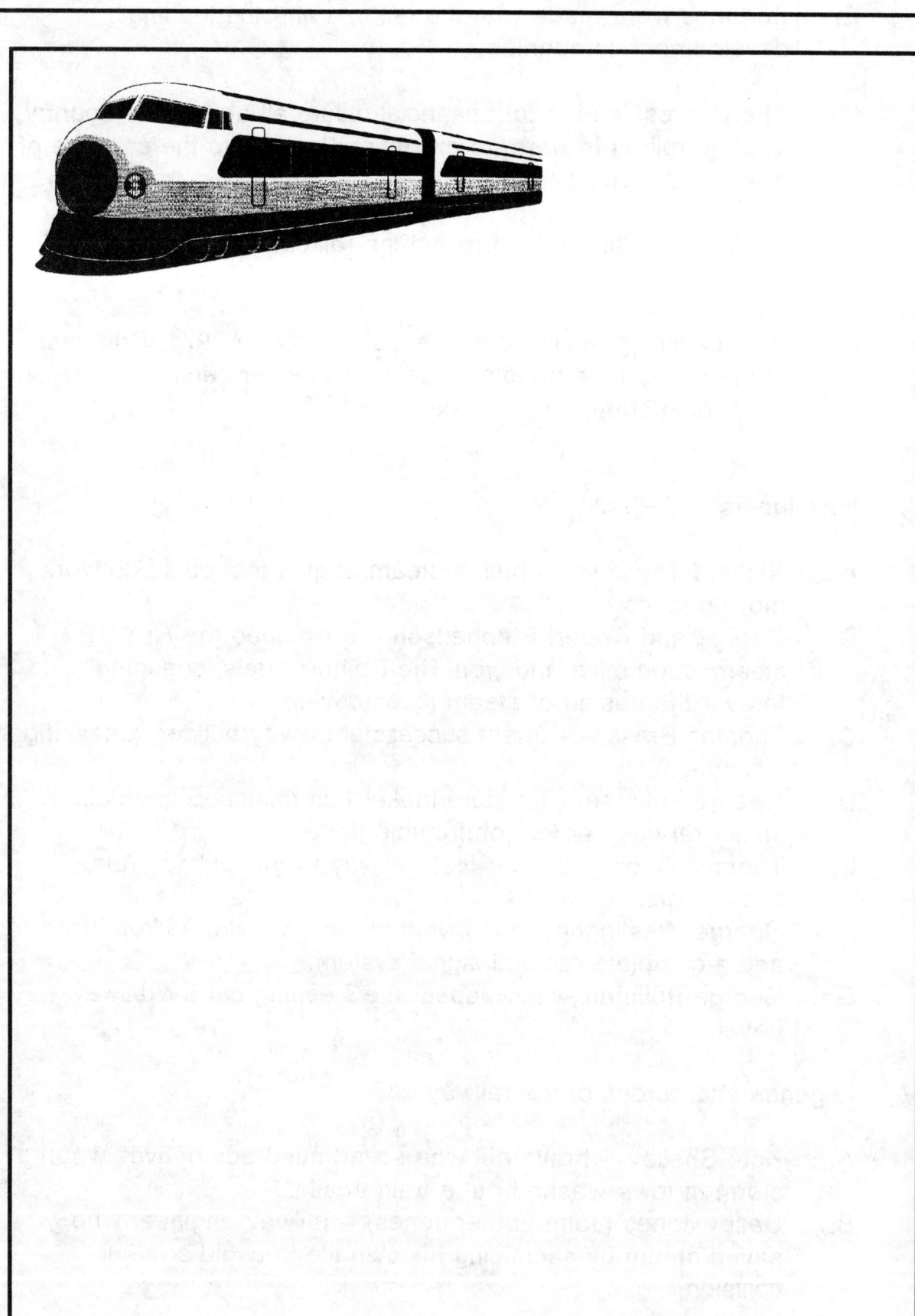

V.   Components of a train

   A.   Engine

      1.   Kinds of engines and how they work
         a.   Steam Engine
         b.   Diesel Engine
         c.   Electric Engine
      2.   Parts of an engine car

   B.   Rolling Stock (Cars)

      1.   Gondola
      2.   Tank
      3.   Coal tender
      4.   Piggy-back
      5.   Refrigerator
      6.   Livestock
      7.   Boxcar
      8.   Hopper
      9.   Auto-rack
     10. Coach
     11. Dining car
     12. Sleeping car

   C.   Caboose

      1.   Purpose
      2.   Parts

   D.   How are the cars connected?

      1.   Coupling Mechanism
      2.   How are the cars switched?

VI.   The Railroad Track

   A.   History of construction
   B.   Gauges of track

TRAINS -- JOB OPPORTUNITIES

Here is a list of some of the jobs that involve trains and railroads:

Train Dispatcher
Train Operator
Tower Operator
Railroad Braker
Train Clerk
Transportation Engineer
Rail Technician
Railroad Clerk
Railroad Inspector
Railroad Maintenance Clerk
Rail Tractor Operator
Rail Surveying Technician
Mechanical Engineer
Electrical Engineer
Conductor
System Engineer
Ticket Agent
Baggage Specialist
Freight Handler

For more information about these jobs or others that may be interesting, go to the reference librarian in the public library and ask for publications in careers. Some that we recommend are:

The Encyclopedia of Careers and Vocational Guidance, published by J. G. Ferguson Publishing Company, Chicago

Occupational Outlook Handbook, published by the US Department of Labor, Bureau of Labor Statistics, presents detailed information on 250 occupations that employ the vast majority of workers. Describes the nature of work, training and educational requirements, working conditions and earnings potential.

TRAINS -- REFERENCE RESOURCES

Here are some of the books that we used to plan and teach this unit. The grade levels listed are from the '93-'94 edition of <u>Books In Print</u> (when available), to give you some idea of the grade level. Use your own good judgement! There are many books available to help with the preparation of a train unit -- look for these and others!

1. **Train Technology**, by Michael Pollard. Technology in Action Series. Grades 5 - 8th. Published by Franklin Watts, Chicago, IL 800 - 672 - 6672.

2. **Tracks Across America**, by Leonard E. Fisher. Grades 5th and up. Published by Holiday House, New York, NY. 212 - 688 - 0085

3. **Train**, Eyewitness Books, by John Coiley. Grades 5th and up. Published by Alfred A. Knopf, New York. 800-733-3000.

4. **Railroads**, by T. Harvey. Grades 3 - 6th. A Question and Answer Book. Published by Lerner Publications, Minneapolis, MN. 800-328- 4929

5. **All Aboard! The Golden Age of American Rail Travel**, edited by Bill Yenne. Published by Barnes & Noble, New York, NY. 800-242-6657.

6. **Railways & Trains**, an Usborne Beginner's Knowledge book, by Caroline Young & Colin King. Grades 2 and up. Published by EDC Publishing, Tulsa, OK 800 - 475 - 4522.

7. **Trains At Work**, by Richard Ammon. Grades 1 - 5th. Published by Macmillan Childrens Group, New York. 800-257-5755.

8. **Steam Locomotives**, by Chris Chant. Grades 3 - 9th. Published by Marshall Cavendish, NY. 800-821-9881.

9. **Rail Travel**, by Alan Cooper. Grades 5 - 9th. Published by Thomson Learning, NY. 212-979-2550.

10. **Trains: The History of Railroads**, by David Jefferis. Grades 5 - 8th. Published by Franklin Watts, Chicago. 800-621-1115.

11. **Trains & Railroads**, from the Read About Science Series. Grades 2 - 6th. Published by Raintree Steck-Vaughn, Milwaukee. 800-558-7264.

12. **Railroaders**, by L. Matthews. Grades 3 - 8th. Published by Rourke Corp., Vero Beach, FL. 407-465-4575.

13. **What It's Like to Be a Railroad Worker**, by Morgan Matthews. Grades K - 3rd. Published by Troll Associates. 800-526-5289.

14. **Steam Train Ride**, by Evelyn Mott. Grades 4 - 8th. Published by Walker & Co., New York. 800-289-2553.

15. **The Story of America's Railroads**, by Spangenburg & Moser. Published by Facts on File, New York. 800-322-8755.

16. **A 19th Century Railway Station: Inside Story**, by Fiona MacDonald and John James. Grades 2 and up. Published by Peter Bedrick Books, New York, NY. 800 - 788 - 3123.

17. **<u>Trains</u>**, A New True Book by R. Broekel. Grades K - 4th. Published by Childrens Press, Chicago, IL 800 - 621 - 1115.

18. **<u>Train Whistles: A Language in Code</u>**, by Helen Sattler. Published by Lothrop, Lee & Shepard Books, New York, NY. 800 - 843 - 9389.

19. **<u>Train Watchers Guide to North American Railroads</u>**, by George Drury. Published by Kalmbach Publishing Company, Waukesha, WI. 800 - 558 - 1544.

20. **<u>Railroad in American Art: Representation of Technological Change</u>**, by Susan Danly and Leo Marx. Published by MIT Press, Cambridge, MA. 800 - 356 - 0343

TRAINS -- READING RESOURCES

Here are some of the books that we read during our unit
on trains. You can find these and many more, usually through
your public library. We enjoyed some of them so much that
we ordered them for our home library! We have used the
grade information listed in the '93-'94 edition of Books In Print
(when available), to give you some idea of the grade level.
Use your own good judgement!

1. **As Far As Mill Springs**, by Patricia Pendergraft. Grades
    5 and up. Published by Philomel Books, New York, NY.
    800 - 631 - 8571.

2. **Kate Shelley and the Midnight Express**, by Margaret K.
    Wetterer. Grades K - 4th. Published by Lerner
    Publications, Minneapolis, MN 800 - 328 - 4929.

3. **Casey Jones**, by Jan Gleiter and Kathleen Thompson.
    Grades PreSchool - 3rd. Published by Raintree
    Publishers Inc., Milwaukee.

4. **Train Song**, by Diane Siebert. Grades K - 3rd.
    Published by HarperCollins Children's Books, New York,
    NY. 800 - 242 - 7737.

5. **The Long Way Westward**, by Joan Sandin. Grades K -
    3rd. Published by HarperCollins Children's Books, New
    York, NY. 800 - 242 - 7737.

6. **Two Little Trains**, by Jean Charlot. Grades Pre-K - 3rd.
    Published by HarperCollins Children's Books, New York,
    NY. 800 - 242 - 7737.

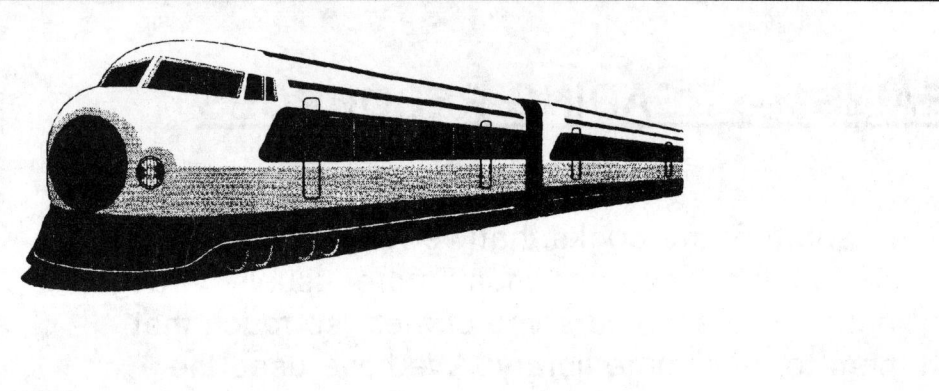

7. **The Train to Lulu's**, by Elizabeth F. Howard. Grades: Preschool - 2nd. Published by Macmillan Childrens Group Books, New York, NY. 800 - 257 - 5755.

8. **The Little Engine That Could**, by Watty Piper. Grades: Preschool - 2nd. Published by Putnam Publishing Group, New York, NY. 800 - 631 - 8571.

9. **Richard Scarry's Trains**, by Richard Scarry. Published by Golden Books.

10. **The Railway Children**, by Edith Nesbit. A family classic, great for reading aloud to all ages. Published by Signet Classic. 800-253-6476.

11. **Across America on an Emigrant Train**, by Jim Murphy. Grades 7 and up. Published by Clarion Books, Houghton Mifflin Company, New York.

TRAINS -- SUGGESTED SPELLING AND VOCABULARY LIST

Lower Level:

train	rail
horn	spike
stack	steel
smoke	track
wheel	tunnel
engine	switch
steam	yard
brake	bridge
cars	station
caboose	lamp
speed	cargo
move	haul
crew	hopper
main	boxcar
line	tank
road	pull
faster	push
roll	trade
safe	flatcar
coach	coal
water	ride
canal	time
boat	ticket
ship	sleep
wagon	dine
horse	board
canoe	trip
river	loud
trail	travel
cowboy	watch

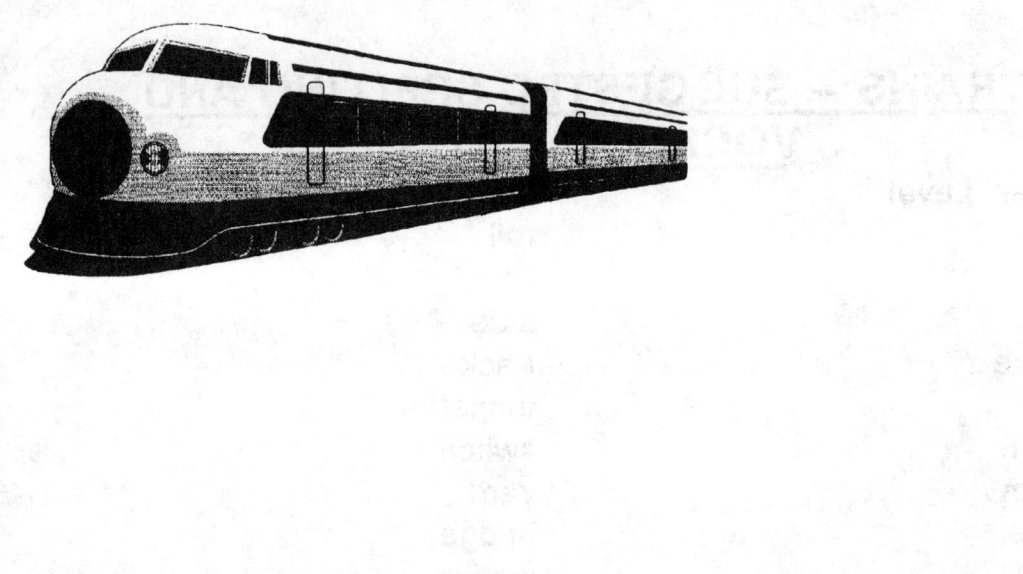

TRAINS -- SUGGESTED SPELLING AND VOCABULARY LIST

Upper Level:

engine

steam

cylinder

pressure

regulator

boiling

locomotive

coal

diesel

controls

caboose

transport

leading

trailing

hopper

livestock

gondola

refrigerator

boxcar

flatcar

passenger

conductor

engineer

brakeman

surveyor

parallel

firemen

route

terminal

dispatcher

telegraph

messages

communicate

connect

transcontinental

electricity

signal

Morse code

telegram

crisscross

reservation

corporation

merger

tycoon

financiers

interstate

commerce

fortune

territory

homesteader

boiler

safety valve

headlamp

smokestack

cowcatcher

whistle

rocker arm

slide rod

tender

feed pipe

TRAINS -- SUBJECT WORD LIST

We have included a list of SUBJECT search words to help you with this unit. To find material about trains and railroads, go to your library's card catalog and look up:

General Topics:
train
railway
locomotive
steam engine
engine
telegraph
transcontinental railway
railroad
rail
diesel train
maglev train
Orient Express
Amtrak
electric train

People:
George Pullman
Robert Stephenson
George Stephenson
Richard Trevithick
James Watt
Rudolf Diesel
George Vanderbilt
Thomas Durant
George Westinghouse
Kate Shelley
Casey Jones

TRAINS -- ACTIVITY RESOURCES

Here are some of the activity books that we enjoyed while studying trains and railways:

1. **Cut and Assemble Old-Fashioned Train**, and
    Easy to Make Train, and
    Antique Locomotives Coloring Book, all available from:

    > Dover Publications, Inc.
    > 31 East 2nd Street
    > Mineola, NY 11501

2   **Great Trains to Cut-Out & Assemble**, published by:

    > Bellerophon Art Books
    > 36 Anacapa St.
    > Santa Barbara, CA 93101
    > (805) 965-7034

3. Look for a train set at garage sales or your local discount store (right after the holidays you can get a great buy!). Develop a layout and begin to build your own railway. There are lots of great guide books for this in the public library, usually in the adult hobby section. The books will show you how to make a layout and assemble it! Great fun to show how trains and railways work!

    You might also want to look for a copy of the magazine **Model Railroader** at the library or news stand for ideas and resources.

TRAINS -- ROOM DECORATION RESOURCES

Consider decorating your "school room" area with train and railroad-oriented items, such as train tickets and schedules, old maps of your county or regional area indicating rail lines (check with your county information office), a model railroad, photos of train engines and travel photos / maps from travel agents and chambers of commerce, along with any free information provided by manufacturers or government agencies! Don't forget a United States map for keeping a good perspective on the immense size of our country and the expanse that the trains had to cover!

Some great posters and pictures can often be obtained by writing to the Public Relations Department of manufacturers of train-related products (Have your reference librarian help you locate these in directories in the reference section, such as Thomas Registers, etc.). When writing various manufacturers, explain that you are preparing to teach a unit on trains and would appreciate any information they can provide.

We wrote to some of the historical societies listed in **Trains** magazine and obtained many free out-of-date calendars that they publish. They had some wonderful train photos, which we used to decorate our room. We also found some old copies of **Trains** magazine at our library's semi-annual sale for 25¢, took them apart and used some of the covers and articles around the room.

Catalog companies that sell train posters, etc. include:

1. Trackside Prints and Hobbies
    Box 690503
    Houston, TX 77269-0503

2.   Scholes Photos
Dept. TM
1423 Kelvin Ct.
Cincinnati, OH 45240

3.   Write to this company for old railroad maps (all states):

Northern Map
ATTN: Dept. TM
11639 Cherokee Circle
Dunnellon, FL 34431-6601

TRAINS -- VIDEO SUGGESTIONS

While learning about trains, our family had the opportunity to view many great shows and videos having to do with trains and the railway. Many of the items listed below can be obtained through your local library or video store.

1. **Love Those Trains**, a National Geographic Video. Outstanding! Available from:

    > National Geographic Society
    > P.O. Box 2118
    > Washington, DC 20013-2118.

2. Reading Rainbow episode, **Trains**. The kids loved this episode.

3. **Union Pacific**, a 1939 video about the race to finish the transcontinental railroad, fantastic scenery and trains. Shown on television from time to time, and also available from libraries and can be ordered from:

    > LocoMotion Pictures
    > 2675 Irvine Ave., Suite F-442
    > Costa Mesa, CA 92627

4. **A Ticket to Tomahawk**, a 1950s family comedy starring Dan Dailey, Anne Baxter, Walter Brennan and Rory Calhoun, and also starring "Emma Sweeney" -- the locomotive Rio Grande Southern No. 20. This film has some terrific railway footage!

Please note: Many of the Reading Rainbow episodes and National Geographic documentary videos are available for loan through the public library system. Ask your librarian for more information.

TRAINS -- FIELD TRIP SUGGESTIONS

There are so many field trips that can be enjoyed while learning about trains, that it is hard to list all of the ones that you might want to consider. Please use this list to get started planning some field trips, then let your imagination identify others that are in your area!

1. Find the closest train station in your area and plan a visit and picnic. Go to spend some time watching the arrivals and departures, freight, types of cars and engines, and count the cars on each train, keeping a journal of your observations. Great way to get a feel for the actual daily operation of the railroad.

2. The best resource that we found for railway and train museums and events was the magazine called **Trains**, published by Kalmbach Publishing (800-533-6644). In each issue, there is a section titled "Directory of Tourist Lines & Rail Museums" that has great field trip information. Get a copy of this magazine at least a month ahead of time so that you have time to write for information for the listings of interest and make field trip plans. The May issue each year has a section that lists recreational train events and excursions for the year.

3. Contact the nearest Railroad Historical Society to get information and plan a field trip for their next meeting/event. Ask your local reference librarian to help you locate the information, or write to **Trains** magazine to obtain a free copy of their list of Historical Societies. Send a self-addressed stamped envelope to:
    > Historical Society List
    > c/o **TRAINS** Editorial Department
    > P.O. Box 1612
    > Waukesha, WI 53187.

TRAINS -- WHAT DO YOU KNOW !??

1.   How much did it cost to build the Erie canal?

2.   What was Casey Jones' real name?

3.   Who developed the four-zone Standard Time system?

4.   What is meant by "consist" when referring to trains?

5.   What was the date of the meeting of the two tracks forming the Transcontinental Railway?

6.   What was a "Zulu Car"?

7.   What was the National Grange of the Patrons of Husbandry (The Grange)?

8.   What is a navvy, when referring to railroads?

9.   Who invented the diesel engine?

10.   What is a semaphore signal?

11. What is a "railroad frog"?

12. What is the measurement between rails for the Standard Gauge in North America?

13. What does Maglev stand for?

14. What is a funicular railway?

15. Where was the first underground railway built?

16. A land agent for the Sante Fe Railway recruited 2,000 wealthy Mennonites to settle in Kansas. From what country did they originate?

ANSWERS -- WHAT DO YOU KNOW !??

TRAINS

1. How much did it cost to build the Erie canal?
    Over seven million dollars.

2. What was Casey Jones' real name?
    **John Luther Jones. He was nicknamed "Casey"
    because he was from Cayce, Kentucky.**

3. Who developed the four-zone Standard Time system?
    **Charles F. Dowd, a teacher, developed the system and
    Congress adopted the system in 1883.**

4. What is meant by "consist" when referring to trains?
    The make-up of the train, in terms of cars.

5. What was the date of the meeting of the two tracks
    forming the Transcontinental Railway?
    They met on May 10, 1869 near Promontory, Utah.

6. What was a "Zulu Car"?
    **The name given to railway cars full of immigrants
    travelling West to take advantage of free transportation
    and low land prices.**

7. What was the National Grange of the Patrons of
    Husbandry (The Grange)?
    **A group formed by midwest farmers to protect their rights
    with the railroad and their freight charges. Their actions
    eventually brought about the formation of the Interstate
    Commerce Commission (ICC) that regulates freight
    rates.**

8. What is a navvy, when referring to railroads?
    A worker on the early railways.

9. Who invented the diesel engine?
    Sir Rudolf Diesel

10. What is a semaphore signal?
    **First used in 1840, it is a railway sign or signal that has
    several wood or metal strips that can be placed in**

various positions to indicate rail condition, activity, etc.

11. What is a "railroad frog"?
The railroad frog was invented by George Westinghouse to let the wheel travelling along the rail of a track to cross an intersecting rail track.

12. What is the measurement between rails for the Standard Gauge in North America?
4 feet 8½ inches, measured from the inside edge of one rail to the inside edge of the other rail.

13. What does Maglev stand for?
Magnetic Levitation -- car hovers above a metal track and is pulled along by magnetic force.

14. What is a funicular railway?
Cable railway that is used in steep areas, mainly to transport tourists.

15. Where was the first underground railway built?
London, England in 1863.

16. A land agent for the Sante Fe Railway recruited 2,000 wealthy Mennonites to settle in Kansas. From what country did they originate?
Russia.

WORKSHEET OUTLINE FOR RESEARCH AND TEACHING NOTES

(Same outline, but increased spacing to provide working and writing room during your unit preparation)

TRAINS -- OUTLINE

I.   History of Transportation in Early America

    A.   Early transportation

        1.   Ocean crossing by sailing ships

        2.   Ships provided transport between coastal

            cities

        3.   Colonists used canoes to travel inland

a.   Colonial transportation

4.   As American colonies grew, roads inland

began to develop.

5.   Covered wagons became the main source of

transportation inland along these rough

roads.

6.   Settlers began crossing the Eastern mountain

ranges, and wagons could not be used for

goods.

7. Pack horses were used along the mountain

trails -- limiting the amount of goods that

could be moved at one time.

B. Early 1800's transportation

1. Improvement of Roads

a. The Lancaster Pike was built -- the first

good road leading to the West.

b. Coastal roads improved for moving

freight -- water transportation was still

more affordable.

2. Water transportation routes were improved

a. Rivers were cleared of barriers

b. Canals were dug for barges to move

goods

c. The Erie Canal was put into service in

1825, connecting the coastal areas to

the inland developments

(1) Four feet deep and forty feet wide

(2) Barges could move freight in one

fourth of the time that wagons

took.

(3) Freight rates dropped from $100

to $5 per ton.

(4) New York City grew rapidly as a

result of this trade access

C. Introducing the steam engine to America

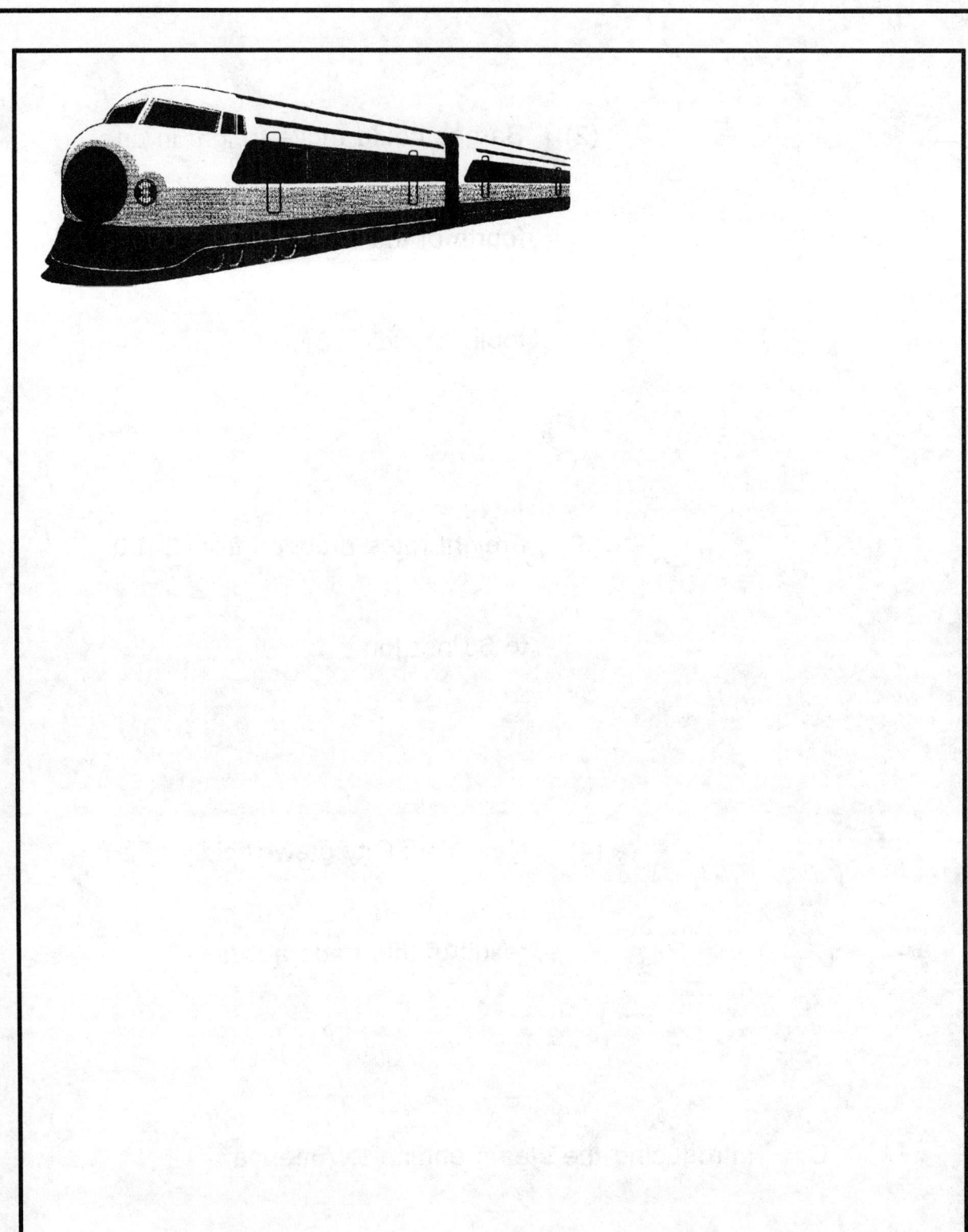

1. Other towns along the coast did not have

    inexpensive inland freight transportation --

    they were limited by mountains and sought

    an alternative.

2. Americans turned to the inventor James Watt

    and his invention -- the steam engine, for a

    way to move goods for less cost.

3. The first steam engine locomotive was used

    to run for a canal company, moving coal.

4.   The first commercial train was put into

service in 1830 in Charleston, South Carolina

by the South Carolina Canal & Railroad

Company.

II.   The railways grow with America

A.   The railways played a major role in America's

Industrial Revolution, providing faster and more

reliable freight transportation, and also fueling rapid

industrial expansion to all parts of our country.

B.	When the Civil War was fought, it marked the first

use of railroads in American conflicts. The

railroads were used to move troops and supplies,

but the South had numerous weaknesses in its rail

system.

C.	The first Transcontinental Railway was completed

in 1869, connecting the Union Pacific and Central

Pacific tracks spanning the continent.

D.   Government land grant program developed to

encourage westward growth and provide the

government with a 50% discount on freight rail

charges.

E.   Fortunes were made with the railroad and the

leading development companies.

F.   The Depression brought financial failure all across

the country, and the railroads were no exception,

leading to the collapse of many of the companies.

G.   The World Wars helped revive the railroad industry

and aid in the recovery of American economy.

H.   With declining mail and passenger service in 1971,

Congress formed Amtrak to handle intercity

passenger service, supporting commuter service.

III. Developers of the railway

    A. Richard Trevithick -- built a steam engine that

       could do work, moving loads

    B. George and Robert Stephenson -- developed the

       ROCKET steam locomotive and won The Rainhill

       Trials, changing forever the design of steam

       locomotives.

    C. Thomas Brassey -- most successful railway builder,

       amassing a fortune.

D. George Pullman -- furniture-maker that designed

and built a luxury railway car for comfortable travel.

E. Thomas Cook -- ran the first "railway excursion" for

train passengers.

F. George Westinghouse -- invented the air brake,

railroad frog, and a complete railroad signal

system.

G. George Pullman -- developed the sleeping car for

railway travel.

IV. Legends and heroes of the railway

A. Kate Shelley -- brave girl who saved hundreds of

lives when a storm in Iowa washed out a train

trestle.

B. Casey Jones (John Luther Jones) -- railway

engineer who saved others by sacrificing his own

life to avoid a major collision.

V.   Components of a train

A.   Engine

  1.   Kinds of engines and how they work

    a.   Steam Engine

    b.   Diesel Engine

    c.   Electric Engine

  2.   Parts of an engine car

B.   Rolling Stock (Cars)

1.   Gondola

2.   Tank

3.   Coal tender

4.   Piggy-back

5.   Refrigerator

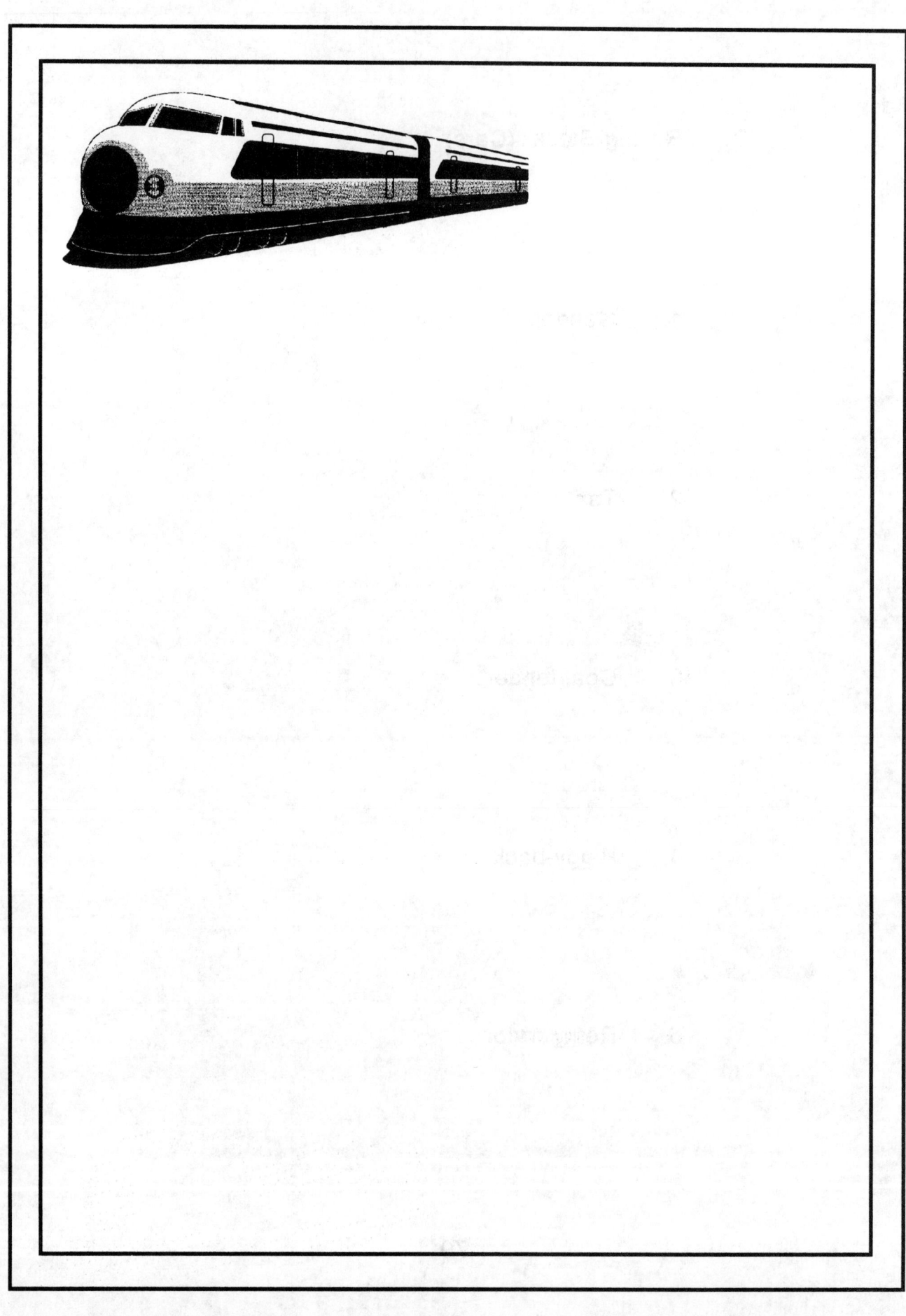

6. Livestock

7. Boxcar

8. Hopper

9. Auto-rack

10. Coach

11. Dining car

12. Sleeping car

C. Caboose

    1. Purpose

    2. Parts

D. How are the cars connected?

    1. Coupling Mechanism

2.	How are the cars switched?

VI.	The Railroad Track

A.	History of construction

B.	Gauges of track

C.	Parts of the track and rail system

D.	Maintenance of the track

VII. Spinoffs of the railway development

A.   Telegraph

B.   Switching and signalling technology

C.   Time zone development and acceptance

VIII. Railway modelling

A.   What does the hobby involve?

B. Layout and plan

C. The train and rolling stock

IX. The railways of today

A. Miles of track over the years of our country's

history

B. Uses of the railway today

C. Future of the railway

1. Maglev trains

2. High Speed trains

ABOUT THE AUTHOR

With a background in engineering and parenting, I am just like my children -- very curious about how things work. They always want to know more, and it is so rewarding to spark their imaginations with topics in technology and nature. With unit studies, I have found that their curiosity gets us through even the longest days.

As this book goes to press, my husband & I are homeschooling our three children. Just like you, we want nothing but the best for our children and have tried several types of curricula. However, we could not find the "right" materials that fit their various interests and learning styles. We decided to create our own unit studies, making them as complete and as interesting as possible. We never intended to publish these, but their popularity and the need that they fill for homeschooling families changed that!

This book is one of a series of science unit studies. The titles currently available include:

Space
Oceans
Flight
Trains

Other titles will be published periodically, as they are written and tested on our own children!